NASCAR *in the Driver's Seat*

By Mark Stewart & Mike Kennedy

Lerner Publications Company/Minneapolis

The publisher wishes to thank science teachers Amy K. Tilmont and Jeffrey R. Garside of the Rumson
Country Day School in Rumson, New Jersey, for their help in preparing this book.

Lerner Publications Company
A division of Lerner Publishing Group, Inc.
241 First Avenue North
Minneapolis, MN 55401 U.S.A.

Website address: www.lernerbooks.com

All photos provided by Getty Images, except for page 19 from author's collection.

Library of Congress Cataloging-in-Publication Data

Stewart, Mark, 1960-
NASCAR in the Driver's Seat / By Mark Stewart & Mike Kennedy.
    p. cm. — (*The Science of NASCAR*)
Includes index.
ISBN 978-0-8225-8737-8 (lib. bdg. : alk. paper)
1. Automobile racing—Juvenile literature. 2. NASCAR (Association)
I. Kennedy, Mike (Mike William), 1965- II. Title.
GV1029.13.S74 2008
796.72—dc22   2007024889

Manufactured in the United States of America
1 2 3 4 5 6 — DP — 13 12 11 10 09 08

Contents

Clap your hands together four times as fast as you can. In the same amount of time, NASCAR drivers must make decisions. Their choices can mean the difference between winning and losing a race. NASCAR drivers study science and math so that they can make good decisions. Every time they enter a race, they are being tested on this knowledge. Often they don't have time to think. They must act fast. This book explores the kind of learning drivers must do before they climb into the driver's seat.

DAVID STREMME
IS READY TO RACE.

LEFT: JUAN PABLO MONTOYA IS SHARP AND FOCUSED BEFORE A PRACTICE RUN. *BELOW:* MATT KENSETH *(LEFT)* AND JEFF BURTON SHARE THEIR IDEAS ABOUT RACING.

Have you ever wondered what driving for a NASCAR team would be like? When you watch races on TV, can you imagine yourself behind the wheel? Every person lucky enough to drive for a NASCAR team says it's a dream come true. They also point out that luck has little to do with winning races. Years of hard work are needed to become a professional driver. That work starts in grade school—when you start training your mind.

FOR DRIVER KYLE BUSCH, THE HARD WORK OF RACING STARTS LONG BEFORE THE RACE ITSELF.

AT NASCAR EVENTS, YOUNG FANS (*ABOVE*) LEARN HOW DRIVERS LIKE KEVIN HARVICK (*RIGHT*) WIN RACES.

THERE IS ALMOST NO ROOM FOR MISTAKES IN A NASCAR RACE!

Know-It-Alls

The people who own NASCAR teams spend a lot of money on their cars. They believe that each victory is a result of planning, hard work, and quick thinking. They expect nothing less than the best. This is especially true when it comes to their drivers. Drivers not only have to be great athletes. They must know how every inch of their car works. They must be able to talk with their teammates about their car's problems. And they must do hundreds of math and science problems in their heads every minute.

LEFT: BOBBY LABONTE GOES OVER EVERY INCH OF HIS CAR BEFORE A RACE. *ABOVE:* KEVIN HARVICK'S PIT CREW HAS TO MOVE FAST AND THINK QUICKLY DURING A PIT STOP.

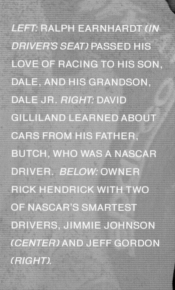

Are modern drivers different from the men and women who drove in the 1950s and 1960s? No, not really. Winning has always taken great courage and a love of cars. That will probably never change. What has changed is that more people are watching NASCAR races than ever before. Drivers must be sure that their cars and crews are ready. They also must meet with their fans and with the people who sponsor their cars. That leaves almost no room for mistakes.

LEFT: RALPH EARNHARDT (*IN DRIVER'S SEAT*) PASSED HIS LOVE OF RACING TO HIS SON, DALE, AND HIS GRANDSON, DALE JR. *RIGHT:* DAVID GILLILAND LEARNED ABOUT CARS FROM HIS FATHER, BUTCH, WHO WAS A NASCAR DRIVER. *BELOW:* OWNER RICK HENDRICK WITH TWO OF NASCAR'S SMARTEST DRIVERS, JIMMIE JOHNSON (*CENTER*) AND JEFF GORDON (*RIGHT*).

Do the Math

A "400" race is 400 miles long. Drivers must do 200 laps to finish the race. How long is each lap?

(answer on page 48)

Bodywork

NASCAR drivers must have strong bodies. On a cool day, the inside of a race car can reach more than 100 degrees. A NASCAR race has no halftime or time-outs. After a driver slips behind the wheel, three hours or more may pass before the driver can rest. Handling a powerful machine takes strong hands, arms, and shoulders. A driver can't say "I'm tired" and rest during a race.

Most drivers work out on the days they are not racing. They lift weights to strengthen their arms and shoulders. They run to build up their endurance (ability to drive for a long time). They do exercises to strengthen their hands. Working in a hot car puts a lot of stress on the heart. (The heart pumps faster to help cool the driver's body.) Drivers have regular checkups with heart doctors to make sure their hearts are working properly. They also talk to diet specialists to make sure they are eating enough of the right foods.

TONY STEWART IS DRENCHED IN SWEAT AFTER A LONG RACE.

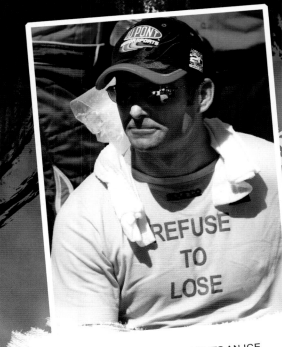

ABOVE: JEFF GORDON PUTS AN ICE BAG ON HIS NECK TO COOL DOWN.
RIGHT: BRIAN VICKERS IS A BIG BELIEVER IN STRENGTH TRAINING.

DAVID GILLILAND USES SPECIAL CUPS TO KEEP HIS HEELS FROM GETTING TOO HOT.

Body Language

The floor of a car gets very hot during a race. There is no way to cool off the floor. Drivers wear specially coated shoes that reflect heat. The coating sends back some of the heat to the floor, so that drivers don't burn their feet.

See for Yourself

The instant NASCAR drivers see something, their brain sends a signal to their body. The signal says, "Take action." How quickly a person acts on the signal is called their reaction time. You can measure your reaction time with this experiment.

- Ask a friend to hold up a yardstick between two fingers. The 36-inches mark should be at the top. The O-inches mark should be at the bottom.
- Sit in a chair. Hold out your hand so that it is even with the bottom of the yardstick. Open your hand wide. Focus your eyes on the part of the yardstick that is directly in front of you.
- Ask your friend to let go of the yardstick, without telling you when.
- Close your hand around the yardstick as soon as you see it move.
- Write down the inch mark at the point you caught the yardstick. This number is your reaction score.

Hold a contest among your friends to see who has the quickest reaction time.

Family Matters

NED *(LEFT)* AND
DALE JARRETT

Have you ever heard the saying "like father, like son"? It means that a special interest or skill may pass from a parent to a child. This is true in NASCAR families. Lee Petty won the first Daytona 500 in 1959. His son Richard won 200 races, including seven Daytona 500s. He was also the NASCAR Sprint Cup Series champion seven times. Dale Earnhardt won the 1998 Daytona 500 and was the NASCAR Sprint Cup Series champion seven times. His son Dale Jr. won the 2004 Daytona 500. Ned Jarrett was the NASCAR Sprint Cup Series champion twice in the 1960s. His son Dale won the title in 1999.

Shoptalk

"PRACTICING WITH HIM AND JUST BEING ON THE TRACK WITH HIM WAS A LOT OF FUN AND JUST REALLY EXCITING."

–DRIVER DALE EARNHARDT JR., ON RACING WITH—AND AGAINST—HIS FATHER

Chapter Two: Draft Day

NASCAR drivers are experts in knowing how air flows around a car. They also know what air passing over the top of one car can do to the cars behind it. This knowledge makes up the science of aerodynamics. On the fastest tracks, a driver can't win or even finish without this knowledge. Air is both the friend and enemy of NASCAR drivers. The more they know about airflow, the more they can use it to their advantage.

A NASCAR RACE IS A LESSON IN AERODYNAMICS.

ABOVE: ONLY A FEW INCHES SEPARATE REED SORENSON AND LEADER KEVIN HARVICK.

RIGHT: SMART RACING HELPED TONY STEWART WIN THE 2007 ALLSTATE 400.

Share the Air

Every driver on the track has one goal—to finish ahead of everyone else. To do so, drivers often must work together. When cars travel at high speeds, the air they pass through resists (pushes back their progress). This air resistance slows down the cars. Their engines must work harder to keep them moving quickly. A hardworking engine uses up fuel faster. By racing single file, several cars can work together to cut down on air resistance. Their engines don't have to work as hard. The cars don't use as much fuel. This allows the cars to stay on the track longer. They can finish laps faster than the other drivers.

CARS RACE INCHES APART AT THE TEXAS MOTOR SPEEDWAY IN FORT WORTH.

Cars that are following close behind each other are drafting. Drafting works because the front car slices through the air. The air then streams over the top and back of the car. If the next driver is following close enough, the air continues over the top and back of the second car. This reduces air resistance. The engine of the second car doesn't have to work as hard to keep up the same speed. The same is true for other cars that join the draft.

TONY STEWART SLIPS BEHIND JEFF GORDON AT TALLADEGA, ALABAMA.

WHEN CARS DRAFT, THE AIR FLOWS SMOOTHLY AROUND THEM.

Do the Math

Let's say a driver can save one gallon of fuel every 25 laps by drafting. How much fuel has the driver saved during a race if the driver drafts for 100 laps?

(answer on page 48)

Leader of the Pack

The first car in a draft works harder than the cars behind it—but not as hard as you might think. This is because greater air pressure is at the front than at the rear of the car. When a car is racing by itself, the high-pressure air at the front "pushes" the car back toward the low-pressure air behind it. When two or more cars are drafting, the low-pressure air does not affect the lead car. The cars racing behind it are pushing the lead car forward.

RIGHT: IN A DRAFT, THE SECOND CAR PUSHES THE LEAD CAR FORWARD. *BELOW:* DRAFTING IS IMPORTANT ON BIG TRACKS LIKE THE DAYTONA INTERNATIONAL SPEEDWAY IN FLORIDA.

THE CARS IN A DRAFT OFTEN RACE LESS THAN A FOOT APART.

Drafting is most important at races, such as the Daytona 500, that are more than a mile long. The tracks for these races are called superspeedways. Crews work hard shaping their cars to cut through the air cleanly and to draft as well as possible. A racing team will often bring its cars to a wind tunnel. These special labs show car designers how tiny changes to a car's shape will work at high speeds.

Show of Force

A race car (left) leaves behind a trail of turbulent (swirling) air. Drivers call this dirty air. It's not actually dirty—just hard to predict. The next time you are in a car that passes a truck on the highway, see if you feel the turbulence of the truck's dirty air.

See for Yourself

What does drafting feel like? Try this experiment the next time you are in a car with the windows rolled down. Remember to tell the driver what you are doing. You'll need the driver's permission and help.

- Cup your hand against the air while the car is moving forward. As the car moves faster, do you feel more or less pressure against your hand? Do you have trouble keeping your hand still?
- Next, tilt your cupped hand downward so the air rushes over the top of it. Do you have to work as hard to keep your hand in place?
- Finally, if your car has a side mirror, place your hand behind it as the car speeds up.
- Move your hand up, down, and back to feel the difference in air resistance.

Think of the mirror as the lead car in the draft. Your hand is the second car. Drivers try to find the spot with the least amount of air resistance.

Air Dale

When it came to drafting, one of the best drivers ever was Dale Earnhardt Sr. (left). He was nicknamed the Intimidator. He got the name partly because he would drive right up to another car's rear bumper. Earnhardt knew the right time to pull behind another car. He had also figured out the best time to make a move on his own. He could read the way air came off of other cars as well as anyone in NASCAR.

Shoptalk

"RACING IS ABOUT BEING THE COOLEST AND THE STRONGEST."

—DRIVER DALE EARNHARDT SR.

DALE EARNHARDT SR. WAS ONE OF THE BEST WHEN IT CAME TO DRAFTING. *TOP:* EARNHARDT *(MIDDLE CAR)* WAITS FOR JUST THE RIGHT TIME TO MAKE HIS MOVE.

Chapter Three: Passing Fancy

Drivers can win a NASCAR race in a number of ways. All ways have one thing in common—passing. The best drivers know how and when to pass. They also know when not to pass.

Good drivers understand that no one likes to be passed. This is especially true when two cars are fighting for the lead. It's also true when one car is about to be lapped. This will result in the car falling a full lap behind. Depending on the size and speed of a track, a driver can try one of several passing moves. Every move requires skill, timing, and respect for the other drivers.

CARL EDWARDS (BELOW) SLIPS PAST MATT KENSETH ON THE INSIDE PART OF THE TRACK.

ABOVE: JEREMY MAYFIELD SQUEEZES BETWEEN
TWO OTHER CARS AT THE DAYTONA 500. BELOW:
JEFF GORDON STREAKS PAST MICHAEL WALTRIP.

Your Turn to Pass

Where is the best place on the track to pass? Many drivers like to wait until they reach the turns before making their move. It is much harder to steer a car through a turn than down the straightaways (the straight sections of a track). On the turns, drivers are more likely to make mistakes, especially when their cars are not handling well. These mistakes create openings for the passing car to slip by.

ROBBY GORDON SQUEEZES BETWEEN DALE EARNHARDT JR. (*TOP*) AND KYLE PETTY (*BOTTOM*).

REED SORENSON (*TOP*) PASSES RYAN NEWMAN ON THE OUTSIDE.

Passing on the straightaways can be difficult too, even when driving a fast car. NASCAR drivers know each other very well. They can guess how, when, and where another driver will try to pass them. They will try to move to that spot and block the passing car. Drivers have only a few seconds to pass between the turns. Passing can be a real guessing game!

Do the Math

To lap another car means to be one whole circuit of the race track ahead. Let's say Matt Kenseth's car laps Ryan Newman's car. How many times must Newman (left) pass Kenseth (right) to finish one lap ahead of Kenseth?

(answer on page 48)

On the Fast Track

At superspeedway races, drafting is an important part of passing. A car leaving the draft to move forward often falls back instead. This is because the car faces sudden air resistance. What happens if a driver wants to get back in line? The others may force that driver to go to the back of the draft. Passing works best when two or three cars leave the draft together. They create a new, smaller draft. Their spotters (team members who watch the race from high above the track) often set up these partnerships. They then radio instructions to their drivers.

ARIC ALMIROLA LEADS THE DRAFT AT THE NASHVILLE SUPERSPEEDWAY IN TENNESSEE.

ABOVE: JAMIE MCMURRAY TAPS KURT BUSCH'S BUMPER. *RIGHT:* A CREW CHIEF WATCHES THE ACTION.

On shorter tracks, the speeds are slower. Drivers find their cars easier to move around or maneuver. Passing on these tracks isn't as risky. A car can pass low on the track or high on the track without losing control. If one car is blocking another, sometimes the passing car will nudge the blocking car's back bumper. This causes the blocking car to slide for just an instant. In the time it takes the driver to regain control, the passing car has pulled ahead. On the more crowded tracks, spotters will tell their drivers whether they are clear to the left and right before they try to pass.

Show of Force

Sometimes a car leaves the draft to pass and no other cars join the move. The air resistance keeps the car from passing and usually pushes the car back in the pack. Drivers call this getting hung out to dry.

See for Yourself

Is it easier to pass high on a turn or low on a turn? That depends on the position of the car you are passing. Given a choice, most drivers prefer to drive the shortest distance when they pass. Which is shorter, high or low? Try this experiment.

- Find two twist ties of equal length.
- Bend the first one into an egg-shaped oval, like some NASCAR tracks. This will be the high part of the track.
- Bend the second twist tie into the same shape. But make sure it fits inside the first one. This is the low part of the track.

The extra length of the second twist tie is the difference between passing high and passing low. Passing low is definitely the way to go!

THESE TWO TWIST TIES ARE EQUAL IN LENGTH. THE RED TWIST TIE SHOWS WHY LOW IS THE WAY TO GO.

Slingshot

One of the most exciting passing moves is the slingshot. A car that has just been passed uses a puff of air from the new leader to whip it back into the lead. As car shapes got smoother and more aerodynamic, this move became harder to pull off. However, the slingshot is still used from time to time. In 2007, Bobby Labonte tried a slingshot pass against his teammate, Tony Stewart, and won the race. Labonte was amazed how well it worked.

Shoptalk

"I'M LIKE, DUDE, THAT WAS A GOOD MOVE!"

—DRIVER BOBBY LABONTE

BOBBY LABONTE *(CENTER)* AND TONY STEWART TALK ABOUT THEIR ONE–TWO FINISH IN A RADIO INTERVIEW.

Chapter Four: Feeling Your Ride

One of the most important things a driver can do when on the track is to tell the pit crew when the car is not running well. A driver knows what every part of the car is supposed to do. If something isn't working right, sometimes the driver can feel it. The driver reports this feeling to the crew. The crew can fix the problem the next time the car comes into the pits.

MICHAEL VALIANTE GETS THE
THUMBS-UP FROM A CREW MEMBER.

ABOVE RIGHT: CREW CHIEF BRAD PARROTT KEEPS AN EYE ON HIS CAR DURING A PRACTICE RUN.

ABOVE LEFT: BOBBY LABONTE DESCRIBES A PROBLEM TO CREW CHIEF PAUL ANDREWS.

BELOW: THE PIT CREW HAS ONLY A FEW SECONDS TO FIX PROBLEMS REPORTED BY A DRIVER DURING A RACE.

Loose and Tight

Drivers often report that their car feels loose. This means that the rear tires are not gripping the track. When a loose car goes through a turn, the driver can feel the car's back end skidding slightly. If the driver doesn't slow down or make a small steering change, the car will spin out. Either way, precious time is lost.

CLINT BOWYER DRIVES INTO THE INFIELD TRYING TO CONTROL HIS SKIDDING CAR.

By Design

Sometimes a car feels tight. The driver senses that the front wheels are skidding as the car goes through a turn. Skidding can be very dangerous, because the rear wheels continue to power the car. A driver must react quickly, or the car could crash into the wall.

When a car is loose or tight, the problem can usually be fixed by making a slight change to the suspension. The car's suspension system spreads a car's weight to its four wheels.

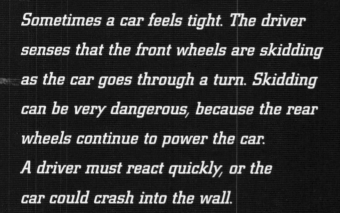

JEFF GREEN HITS THE WALL. HE WAS UNHURT, BUT HIS CAR WAS UNABLE TO STAY IN THE RACE. *BELOW:* MARCOS AMBROSE TESTS HIS CAR BEFORE A RACE AT WATKINS GLEN, NEW YORK.

Practice Makes Perfect

Before a race, NASCAR drivers practice. But they don't practice their driving skills. They use the practice time to get a feel for how their cars will run on the track. The crew depends on the driver to report all problems.

KASEY KAHNE (*LEFT*) AND ELLIOTT SADLER (*CENTER*) MEET WITH TEAM OWNER RAY EVERNHAM.

The crew makes repairs or adjustments (changes). Then the driver takes the car back onto the track for a few more laps. If the problem is fixed, the crew works on ways to make the car ride smoother and faster. Sometimes these changes create new problems. The driver and crew must put their heads together again to fix them. By race day, car and driver should be ready to roll.

JEFF PRUETT (*LEFT*) DISCUSSES A PRACTICE RUN WITH TWO CREW MEMBERS.

In a Flash

NASCAR drivers are always talking during practice, and someone is always listening. In fact, sometimes hundreds of people are! Many fans bring portable scanners to the track. They can listen as their favorite drivers talk with their crews.

See for Yourself

What does a NASCAR driver feel when a car is slightly out of balance? Try this experiment.

- Slip on your school backpack, and walk down a long path or hallway.
- Pay close attention to the way the straps rest on your shoulders and press against your back.
- Remove the backpack.
- Turn away while a friend hides a rock or something else that weighs about one pound in one of the pack's side pockets.
- Slip the pack back on, and walk down the path or hallway again.

Does the pack feel different?
Can you guess where the extra weight is?

Talk to Me

"WHEN YOU GET TWO PEOPLE WITH THE SAME DESIRE AND THE SAME PASSION, YOU ALWAYS FIND A WAY OF WORKING WELL TOGETHER."

–CREW CHIEF GREG ZIPADELLI (WITH DRIVER TONY STEWART)

Shoptalk

Chatter is what racing fans call the radio talk between driver and crew chief during a race. Here's an exchange between Dale Earnhardt Jr. and Tony Eury. DE: "It's real, real tight…There['s] no way I can get through turn one. I've tried every way I can." TE: "We could change a shock, but I don't wanna lose all that track position." After the shock was changed during a pit stop, Dale remarked, "Yeah! It's way better, way better now."

Sometimes a car has a problem during a race. The driver and crew chief must be able to talk about it quickly and clearly. Good communication can make the difference between winning and losing. When a driver is cool headed and quiet, like Mark Martin or Ricky Rudd, fixing problems is easy. Some drivers, including Dale Earnhardt Jr. and Tony Stewart, are easily excited. They need calm crew chiefs who can get to the heart of the problem fast. Earnhardt chose his cousin, Tony Eury Jr., to be his crew chief.

Chapter Five: Every Second Counts

The Michigan International Speedway in Brooklyn, Michigan, measures exactly two miles around. The NASCAR races held there usually are 200 laps. At the end of a 400-mile race, only a few seconds may separate the winner and the runner-up. How does one car gain those precious seconds over the others? This is where teamwork comes in. On race day, everyone is focused on the clock.

DENNY HAMLIN'S PIT CREW WORKS FAST. IT TAKES TEAMWORK TO WIN A RACE.

RIGHT: CARL EDWARDS *(CENTER STANDING)* CELEBRATES AFTER A RACE. EVERYONE ON HIS TEAM SHARES IN HIS VICTORIES. *BELOW:* QUICK WORK IN THE PITS PAYS OFF FOR JAMIE MCMURRAY. HE REACHES THE FINISH LINE AN INSTANT BEFORE KYLE BUSCH.

Easy Does It

A skilled pit crew takes between 15 and 20 seconds to change a set of tires during a pit stop. Naturally, drivers don't want to change their tires more than they have to. Then again, they don't want to drive too long on the same tires. Tires wear out faster as they heat up. If a tire wears down too far, it can blow apart and a car could crash. A driver and crew need to decide how they can get through a race without changing tires more often than the other teams. Making tires last is one way to make every second count.

BRIAN VICKERS STOPS FOR NEW TIRES AND MORE FUEL DURING A RACE AT THE TEXAS MOTOR SPEEDWAY.

ABOVE: JIMMIE JOHNSON BLOWS A TIRE.
BELOW: CASEY MEARS (LEFT) AND CREW CHIEF
JIMMY ELLEDGE CHECK THE WEAR ON A TIRE.

In the Mix

NASCAR teams have many different tire choices. The blend of each tire's rubber compound is slightly different. The goal is to find the right tire for each track a team visits during the season.

Another way drivers can save time is by being gentle with their engines. A racing engine is built to last for 500 miles or more. However, a careless driver can push an engine past its limits. Driving too hard early in a race can cause the delicate parts of an engine to wear out near the end. The longer the race, the more careful teams must be. Some engine problems can be fixed during pit stops. But if an engine blows, the race for that team is over.

Fuel for Thought

If everything is going as planned in a race, the only reason a car absolutely needs to pit stop is for more fuel. A racing team knows how far its car can run before it needs to refuel. On a short track, it might be once every 100 laps. On a longer track, a car may only go 50 laps before the tank runs dry. The goal is to spend as little time refueling as possible.

MATT KENSETH'S CREW REFUELS HIS CAR DURING THE DAYTONA 500.

Sometimes a disabled car or car parts create a hazard on the track. In this case, race officials wave a yellow caution flag. This is a signal for the drivers to slow down. Many cars refuel and change tires during a caution period. With everyone on the track going slowly, they lose less time while they are in the pits. When a caution flag comes out near the end of a race, some cars take on only the fuel they need to finish a race. They don't change their tires. This pit stop takes less than ten seconds and is called a "splash and go."

NASCAR TEAMS RELY ON COMPUTERS TO HELP THEM STUDY FUEL USE.

Do the Math

Let's say a NASCAR team makes six pit stops. Each pit stop lasts 15 seconds. How long has the car been at rest during the race?

(answer on page 48)

See for Yourself

Tires wear out faster as they heat up. If a track is smooth, tires will stay at a lower temperature. If a track is rough, they tend to get hot fast. Try this experiment to understand how friction—the rubbing of one surface against another—and heat are linked.

- Identify three different surfaces—a smooth sheet of paper, the skin on your own forearm, and rough carpeting.
- Rub your hand over each as fast as you can for five seconds. Note which surface creates the most heat.
- Rub your hand over each again as fast as you can for 10 seconds.
  Note that the rougher the surface, the warmer the surface gets.
- Rub your hand over each for 10 seconds but push down harder on each surface this time. The carpet gets very hot. Your forearm is a bit hot. The paper is hardly hot at all.

Which surface do you think is most like a rough track?

Running on Empty

Even the smartest racing teams mess up the math once in a while. In 2006, teammates Greg Biffle (above right) and Mark Martin (above left) *were* running second and fourth at the Phoenix International Raceway. Both had a chance to win with two laps to go. Both ran out of gas! Their crew chiefs were angry and embarrassed. Team owner Jack Roush was not very happy either.

"WE HAD PROBABLY TWO OF THE BEST CARS!"

—TEAM OWNER JACK ROUSH

NASCAR drivers are more than fast and fearless athletes. They are great learners too. They are hungry for knowledge, because this is truly the difference between success and failure. The more they know about their cars, their crew members, and the other drivers, the greater their chance of winning.

Glossary

aerodynamics: the science of how air flows around an object

air resistance: the force of air pushing against a moving object

air turbulence: the force created by swirling air

drafting: racing closely in single file to reduce the effect of air resistance. At high speeds, drafting can lower the amount of energy needed to keep up a certain speed.

lap: one circuit around a track; to be ahead of another car by one entire circuit of the track

NASCAR: the National Association for Stock Car Auto Racing

passing: going by a moving car to get in front of it

pit crew: the seven-member team that takes care of a race car during a race. The crew chief leads the pit crew.

reaction time: the time it takes for a person to act on a signal from the brain

sponsor: the group or person who pays money to support a racing team

superspeedway: a circular track that is more than one mile long

suspension system: the springs, shocks, and other parts that are used to suspend (hang) a car's frame, body, and engine above the wheels

Learn More

Books

Buckley, James. *NASCAR*. New York: DK Eyewitness Books, 2005.

Buckley, James. *Speedway Superstars*. Pleasantville, NY: Reader's Digest, 2004.

Doeden, Matt. *Stock Cars*. Minneapolis: Lerner Publications Company, 2007.

Fielden, Greg. *NASCAR Chronicle*. Lincolnwood, IL: Publications International, Ltd., 2003.

Sporting News. *NASCAR Record & Fact Book*. Charlotte, NC: Sporting News, 2007.

Woods, Bob. *The Greatest Races*. Pleasantville, NY: Reader's Digest, 2004.

Woods, Bob. *NASCAR Pit Pass: Behind the Scenes of NASCAR*. Pleasantville, NY: Reader's Digest, 2005.

Website and Video Game

NASCAR
http://www.nascar.com
NASCAR.com is the official site of NASCAR.
From here you can find information on drivers and their teams, as well as previews of upcoming races, schedules, and a look back at NASCAR's history.

NASCAR 2008. Video game. Redwood City, CA: EA Sports, 2008.
With an ESRB rating of E for "everyone," this game gives fans a chance to experience the speed and thrills of driving in a NASCAR race.

Index

aerodynamics, 14, 16, 26–27, 29
air resistance. *See* aerodynamics

car problems, 8, 30–37
car shape, 19
caution period, 43
chatter, 37
crew chiefs, 37, 45

Daytona 500, 13, 19, 42
dirty air, 19
drafting, 16–21, 26
drivers, 4, 8–9, 10, 14, 24, 27, 34, 41, 45

Earnhardt, Dale, Jr., 13, 37
Earnhardt, Dale, Sr., 13, 21
Eury, Tony Jr., 37

fans, 9, 35, 37
friction, 44
fuel, 16, 42–43, 45

Michigan International Speedway, 38

NASCAR drivers: Ambrose, Marcos, 33; Biffle, Greg, 45; Bowyer, Clint, 32; Jarrett, Dale, 13; Jarrett, Ned, 13; Kenseth, Matt, 25; Labonte, Bobby, 29; Martin, Mark, 37, 45; Newman, Ryan, 25; Petty, Lee, 13; Petty, Richard, 13; Rudd, Ricky, 37; Stewart, Tony, 29, 37. *See also* Earnhardt, Dale, Sr.; Earnhardt, Dale, Jr.
NASCAR racing teams, 6, 8, 19, 38–39, 42, 45

passing, 22–24, 26–29
Phoenix International Raceway, 45
pit crews, 9, 30–31, 34–35, 38, 40
pit stops, 40–43

racing team. *See* NASCAR racing team
reaction time, 12

skidding, 32–33
slingshot pass, 29
"splash and go," 43
spotter, 26–27

team owners, 8, 34, 45
tires, 40–41, 43, 44
training, 4, 6, 10, 34

Do the Math Answers

Page 9: 2 miles. 400 miles ÷ by 200 laps = 2 miles per lap.
Page 17: 4 gallons. 100 laps ÷ by 25 laps = 4 x 1 gallon = 4 gallons.
Page 25: Twice. Once for Newman to get on the same lap as Kenseth, and once more to pull ahead of him.
Page 43: 90 seconds. 6 stops x 15 seconds per stop = 90 seconds.